Stopping by the Side of the Road

A Tale about Dying

Stopping by the Side of the Road

A Tale about Dying

Jody Whelden

Illustrations by Ann Thomas

RADIANT HEART PRESS
Milwaukee, Wisconsin

This book is a work of fiction that depicts no real people, but draws on the experiences of many.

Published by Radiant Heart Press,
an imprint of HenschelHAUS Publishing, Inc.
www.henschelHAUSbooks.com

ISBN: 978159598-393-0
E-ISBN: 978159598-394-7
Audio ISBN: 978159598-395-4 (CD)
Audio ISBN: 978159598-402-9 (MP3)

Library of Congress Control Number: 2015933749

Publisher's Cataloging-In-Publication Data
(Prepared by The Donohue Group, Inc.)
Whelden, Jody.
Stopping by the side of the road : a story about dying / Jody Whelden ;
illustrations by Ann Thomas.
pages : illustrations ; cm
Issued also as an ebook and an audiobook.
ISBN: 978-1-59598-393-0
1. Death--Psychological aspects. 2. Terminally ill--Psychology. 3. Loss (Psychology)
4. Conduct of life. 5. Adjustment (Psychology) I. Thomas, Ann, 1949- II. Title.
BF789.D4 W44 2015
155.9/37   2015933749

Author photo: Adam Karl Photography

Printed in the United States of America.

This book is dedicated to my parents,

Edith Irwin Whelden and

John Eaton Whelden,

who taught me to use my gifts and my grit.

Preface

In my late twenties, I sat on a hillside in Vermont. I had a master's degree, a good job, good friends, and a comfortable life. It was not enough for me. I was restless and unsatisfied. I sat with a troubled heart and asked myself, "What is the right way to live life?"

The answer came like a boomerang, "Find the answer to the question—*What is true power?*"

With lightning speed, I had found my rudder, my true North. This question has been my life raft when I find myself overboard in a rough sea. Finding answers to this question has propelled me through life.

The central answer? True power is the power within and acting on its wisdom. This knowing and my inner compass led me to create this book and put it into the world.

In 2013, I began a major transformation of consciousness and direction. I now strive to live from my heart and body and my highest self in accord with "the great source," which is known by many names and experiences. I hope to be of service to others in multiple ways.

Among other things, I will be writing books, starting with this one. This book came to me in a dream in 2008. The dream instructed me to publish "stories like this." I did record it, but did not publish it until the right time—which is now. Some commonly asked questions about the book (and their answers) are provided at the end of the book. I thought you'd enjoy reading the story first. Feel free to peek if you prefer.

With love, Jody
Madison, Wisconsin, 2015

Conversation-guiding questions are also included at the end of the book. They are there if you would like to use them for yourself or with others.

Acknowledgments

For their support and major contributions to this book I say thank you—with great gratitude—to:

- Illustrator Ann Thomas, whose magnificent talent has rendered the spirit of this story so beautifully in visual art;

- Publisher Kira Henschel, whose grace and vision has reliably brought me and this story every step of the way;

- Editor Laura Holliday, master wordsmith, whose clarity and passion added so much value to the story;

- Painter, Consultant, and Teacher Marcia Jones, whose endless capacity to inspire and nurture the artistic soul gave me enduring gifts as I created the templates for the illustrations;

- Sound engineer Neal Ewers, whose deep, experienced skill and thoughtfulness created the audio version of this story.

- My sister, Rebecca Whelden Hagerty, whose magnificent presence in the world harbors me as only she can;

- Evolutionary sister Vida Groman, whose presence in the world inspires me as only she can;

- And to all other friends and family who have given me feedback, support, and ideas. I could not be publishing this without your wisdom, love, and strength.

Stopping by the Side of the Road

A Tale about Dying

The rose bushes needed pruning—except I couldn't reach the right branches; my back was stiff where it used to be limber. I stretched and tried again. The headache from last night lingered, my chest braced against intermittent needle-sharp jabs, and my emotions elbowed each other like odd-shaped glass jars in a box.

As I groaned to relieve the pressure of the work, an invisible whisperer suggested a ride in the countryside. I agreed.

Windows down, I drove out of town and into the sunny day. I smelled the fields, watched a flying hawk, and enjoyed the anthem of a farmer's tractor. A roadside brook somersaulted into crests of whites and dove into deep blues.

After a while, up ahead, I saw a dirt road pushing its way through flowering bushes. I turned off the pavement and onto the tamped-down earth.

The undisturbed woods filled my senses; dust kicked and ran at the heels of the car. The trees' canopy protected texture, light, and sound. Bush, tree, flower and bird, animal and insect, moved in a secret rhythm. My breath came easier.

Then, around a bend, a small stone chapel appeared, standing back from the road and tucked into its surroundings as if it had grown there. Red brick accented rough stonework, and flat-topped windows rose narrow and tall on either side of wide double doors. Purple and yellow wildflowers speckled the grass.

I stopped by the side of the road to see if I could get in. Climbing out of the car, stiff from the drive, I wondered when the last visitor had been there.

As I approached the doors, an old cemetery came into view, tucked around the corner of the chapel, the irregular headstones scratched with old epitaphs.

I found the doors locked. The chapel smiled its silent resolve. I sat on a sun-warmed boulder and breathed in sweet air. Across the road, the morning sun laughed and played with the tops of the flowers and grasses. Most of my pains were gone.

As my muscles softened in the sun, a young woman came walking down the road. She wore a long gold and white summer dress and a straw hat with ribbons. Her walk, her manner, were ageless. When she got to me, sitting on my rock, she took off her hat, releasing long, dark hair to tumble around her face.

She cupped her hand over her eyes and smiled. "Are you wanting to get in the chapel?"

At first, her approach had felt like an intrusion, but now, feeling her authentic concern, I relaxed. "Well, yes," I said. "I think it's locked, though."

"I can get you in." Not waiting for my reply, she smiled and pulled a large skeleton key from her pocket. "Come along," she invited, turning and beckoning to me.

At the door, the woman pushed the key into the keyhole. I heard the clink of the lock opening, then a deeper thunk as the latch released.

"There you go. I'll come back and lock it." She returned the key to her pocket.

With wonder, I watched her go. It was like being in a dream. She came, just when I needed her; then, there she went. She was so self-contained and at ease. She needed nothing from me. Her steps were light, her sun-checkered back swaying in the light and shadow.

The chapel door stood ajar and I stepped over the threshold. Sunlight slanted through the dust-covered windows and made splotches on the old floorboards. High-backed wooden chairs lined the walls; they seemed to be anticipating a dance to be held at any moment. A simple oak lectern stood at the front of the chapel, and the walls held a pale blue paint with white trim.

I sat on a chair and scanned the quiet room. It smelled stale. The only fresh air came in the open door.

I daydreamed for a while, losing track of time. Memories appeared like pages in an old book. I didn't choose them; they chose me. Colors, emotions, and sounds brightened or darkened the pictures. One memory brought tears; I laughed at another; one led me to stillness.

After a while, with a tender touch, the memories whispered away.

I sensed the woman in the chapel doorway. How long had she been there, watching me? She smiled and leaned on the door jamb, both hands holding the brim of her hat. No need to guard her eyes from the sun this time.

"You can say a few words if you want." She gestured toward the lectern. "I came to listen."

When I didn't move right away, she added, "Why don't you try and see what happens? It's just you and me."

Her slow, sweet smile matched her eyes, kind and strong. My curiosity pulled me in; I couldn't resist. Again, my annoyance fell away.

"Okay," I finally said, standing and walking to the lectern. I pushed it around until I felt settled. I cleared my throat.

My words staggered out. "Um … well. Let's see. I have to say, I'm really not too sure what's going on." I laughed awkwardly, a short, abrupt sound. "I mean, the longer I'm here, the more I realize that this is a—a new kind of experience for me."

ealizing the truth of those words, I continued. "I mean, I can feel—yeah—this is really quite unusual. It's weird, but—I don't mean in a bad way, really. I mean … it seems even kind of special—or maybe even very important … but I really don't know what to think." My chest tightened, and that scared me. My mind went blank.

"I can't think of anything to say," I said, my throat dry and my body numb. I repeated, "Really, there's nothing I can think of to say."

Not wanting to appear ungrateful, I added, "But thanks for letting me in. It's really very pretty. And ... I think ... I think I should be going now."

My body organized itself to leave. However, I felt the desire to stay. I wondered, *Why not stay a little longer? Why am I so nervous? And who is she, anyway?*

As soon as I had these questions, I didn't need to ask them out loud. The answers had a relentless presence—but as yet unclear. My curiosity wanted to pursue them, like wanting to dig one's toes into thick green grass and the dirt beneath. You knew it would be satisfying—but it might be messy, too.

The woman came in and sat down. Jarred by her movement, I fled into my inner reasoning once again, telling myself, *This is silly. There are things I need to do at home.*

However, on the edge of the desire to flee, those unrelenting answers beat a rhythm. My eyes closed. I hesitated, grasping at the lectern and cloaking myself in courage to listen to that message. I had to follow the beat.

The truth arrived like a wave on the beach—
natural, forceful and gentle. I knew what was
happening. Those aches and pains I'd been
having made sense. I was stunned with initial disbelief,
but relieved to know what was happening. My eyes
teared. The choice I had was where I wanted to be: I
could either drive back to town or stay here.

I stayed.

As I came alert, the room was familiar now, a comfort.

With my blurry gaze on the sunlit floorboards, I asked, "Is this what I think it is?"

"Well, I think it might be," she replied. Her tone comforted, even if the words did not.

I asked another way: "I mean, do I have to go right now?" I looked up, but my voice dropped to a whisper. "I don't really think I'm ready. It seems too soon."

efore she could answer, my inner dialogue began again. It was another reasoned argument, this time about how this could not be happening.

But soon the chatter quieted, like it does in a theater when the house darkens, the curtain rises, and light fills the stage. The actors became visible in my mind. The characters interacted with each other, sorting out their dilemma and coming to a resolution. My face felt a slow smile of its own. My heart stopped racing; my muscles fit my body better.

cleared my throat. "I mean, I don't know what I thought it would be like. It is such a surprise."

The time had come to be bold. I said, "I—I do believe—really, I think—I am probably dying. Is that right?"

She did not answer me.

I paused and said, "Well, I mean ... I believe—I am dying."

had a surprise then. I didn't feel terrible saying those words. Instead, calmness filled me. Her presence reassured me that I had all the time I wanted. I moved from one foot to the other, feeling the shift, like an ocean liner trimming its tabs and going a new direction—a subtle adjustment leading to a big change.

First, I knew I wouldn't speak with my loved ones again. I saw them all, their faces beaming in rich colors. Each had so much beauty and held precious gifts. Grief rushed through me.

Then, like a rainbow after a storm, the love I shared with each of them came in beautiful, colorful waves. I realized that nothing real—like that love—would be destroyed by my death.

And then the mundane arrived. I thought of my home. *Who would get the new chair? What about my favorite painting? And who had I told about my papers?* I felt silly having these thoughts, but then realized they were natural. More concerns tumbled in: *would the indoor plants find new homes? Maybe someone would cherish my mother's clock*—I hoped so.

I knew I had done some good and won some battles. Did anyone know how hard I had fought? With hope, love, and friends, I had found my way. I saw the lost struggles—and my failures of integrity or clouded vision. I forgave myself for most. I knew all these things had their place.

Next came the times of fun and pleasure, and those memories made me happy again—fabulous happiness! Those formless gems lived as strong as any diamond in my heart.

My estranged brother came to mind; I sent him love. I forgave him—would he forgive me? I wished we had found a way to reconciliation.

Thinking of my brother led me to thinking of the great unseen dimension of life—the invisible choreography. I had wrestled so many times to understand the eternal, the infinite, God, or, as some said, the essence, the source of life, the Mother. I had arrived at my own personal understanding a while ago, clear sometimes and sometimes unclear—but never in doubt anymore.

ow, I rested in that comfort, letting it soothe my inner spaces.

I drifted inward one last time. An inner chorus began chanting "Thank you, thank you ..." The chorus sang to me and I sang to it. The beautiful chant now had music. *Thank you, I love you, I forgive you, thank you.* The chorus and I sang outside of time, matching one another's pitch and tone. Then, the chant disappeared gently, behind my heart.

Becoming present in the room once again, I watched as the beauty of the room danced with the beauty of nature coming in the windows. That beauty had been there all the time, I realized; I was just letting myself experience it for the first time.

Out loud, I said one more thing: "I am so grateful for it all."

Then, I looked up to find her. The young woman had left the chapel, but I could see her through the open doors, walking toward the field opposite the building.

Sensing her invitation, I started toward her, lingering for a moment to touch the edge of the lectern, enjoying the grain of the wood. Then I put my hands in my pockets and left the chapel.

The sun sat high in the sky. Insects and birds flew; animals scampered across the ground and rustled in the underbrush. The woman waited for me on the other side of the road. The movement of the breeze was comforting.

When I got to her, she placed her arm in mine, and our flesh warmed each other. In silence, we walked further into the field.

Behind us, I heard the chapel door shut and the latch click.

I began to feel lighter and lighter. Her wordless, loving presence held me—and let me go. I felt an eagerness I had not expected.

Now, my feet just skimmed the earth. I lifted above the beautiful field. My edges dissolved and my being joined with the peaceful, brilliant, all-surrounding love.

Questions

If you would like to have a conversation with a friend or loved one, or gather with a group and discuss this story, here are some questions you might use.

- What memories or thoughts did you experience while you read or listened to the story?

- Have you ever come close to dying? What can you share about that experience? How has that experience left you feeling about dying?

- Have you ever thought about the process of dying? What?

- Have you seen or been with anyone when he or she was dying? What was difficult about your experience? What was glorious about your experience?

- Have you ever thought about how you would like your death to be? What have you thought? Or, why do you think you have not thought about it?

- Have you had a vision or premonition about your death? Have you ever had a premonition about someone else's death?

- In the story itself, do you identify with either of the characters. Whom do you like or don't like? What would you have wanted to be different?

- Whom would you want to talk with once you know you are dying? What would you like to talk about?

- Have you done any planning for your death? Does your family know what you want? Have you discussed it with your children/adult children? Why or why not?

- Where do you want to be when you die and whom do you want there?

- What other thoughts have you been having about dying?

Author's Comments

The questions I am most often asked about this book are:

Who is this book for?

My answer has always been, "I don't know." The dream did not make that clear. Since I have been sharing this story with others, the brief tale seems to appeal to so many people for different reasons. I hope it can be of use to individuals and families, to professionals serving the dying. Please let me know who it has helped. I would love to answer this question more clearly someday.

What came to you in the dream and what have you added?

The woman driving, stopping by the side of the road to see the chapel, the "guide," and the ensuing specific events before the drive and many of the main character's inner thoughts have been added.

Is any of this your own experience or what you expect for yourself?

This story is not about any particular experience of my own, nor one I am anticipating, necessarily (since we never know!)

I have been a hospital chaplain since 2002 and have had the honor of being present with many dying people. This story does reflect those experiences, and those I have had with my own loved ones.

What did you learn from writing this story?

I now know the gift of presence and peace is possible when the time comes to accompany ourselves or our loved ones over the threshold. May it be so.

About the Author

Rev. Jody Whelden, RBCC, is a Unitarian Universalist Community Minister and a Retired Board Certified Chaplain. She has worked in the healing arts since 1974, when she was a high school guidance counselor in New Hampshire and Vermont, which she still visits. In recent years, she has lived and worked in Wisconsin and Pennsylvania. She has been a hospital chaplain, religious educator, consulting parish minister, group educator, psychotherapist, learning consultant, and counselor. She can be reached through her website, www.jodywhelden.com.

www.ingramcontent.com/pod-product-compliance
Lightning Source LLC
Chambersburg PA
CBHW040033050426

42453CB00003B/99

9781595983930